The
Crafty Art
Book

Jane Bull

LONDON, NEW YORK, MUNICH,
MELBOURNE, AND DELHI

DESIGN • Jane Bull
TEXT • Penelope Arlon
PHOTOGRAPHY • Andy Crawford
DESIGN ASSISTANCE • Sadie Thomas

PUBLISHING MANAGER • Sue Leonard
MANAGING ART EDITOR • Clare Shedden
PRODUCTION • Shivani Pandey
DTP DESIGNER • Almudena Díaz

For Charlotte, Billy, and James

First American Edition, 2004
Published in the United States by
DK Publishing, Inc., 375 Hudson Street,
New York, New York 10014
04 05 06 07 08 10 9 8 7 6 5 4 3 2 1

Library of Congress Cataloging-in-Publication Data

Bull, Jane, 1957-
  The crafty art book / written by Jane Bull.-- 1st American ed.
    p. cm.
  ISBN 0-7566-0550-4
  1. Handicraft--Juvenile literature. I. Title.
TT160.B86 2004
745.5--dc22

2004002341

ISBN: 0-7566-0550-4

Color reproduction by
GRB Editrice S.r.l., Verona, Italy
Printed and bound in China by Toppan

discover more at
www.dk.com

Get crafty
with your art

A crafty book of arty ideas . . .

to make perfect gifts...

for family and friends

Ha Ha

Crafty kit • Here's a guide to the materials

Paper or cardboard?

TRACING PAPER • You will need tracing paper for the Pirate Pete templates; however, parchment paper is a great alternative.

TISSUE PAPER • Tissue paper is the best paper for the roses.

PAPER • Normal, everyday paper can be used for the marble and other printing techniques.

CARD • Folded boxes can be made with paper or very thin posterboard. Paper is easier to fold and surprisingly sturdy. Thin posterboard is best for woolly web bases and for cards and tags.

Tissue paper

Paints and pens

POSTER PAINT • It is a good all-around paint for posterboard and paper. It is cheap and easy to use. For printing paper, use poster paint.

OIL PAINT • When you make the marble paper, you will need to use oil paint. You will also need some turpentine—ask your parents to help you with this.

FABRIC PENS • When you use fabric pens to decorate Pirate Pete, follow the instructions on the packet for best results.

Poster paint

Bits and pieces

To finish off your projects nicely, you will often need odds and ends. Keep a lookout at home for things that are about to be thrown away and start collecting for your arty crafts. Look for items such as: .

*   Buttons and beads
*   Ribbon
*   Old paper
*   Things to print with, like empty thread spools, used-up pens, old sponges, and anything else with good texture.

☆ **Ask an adult.** You will see this sign if you need to ask an adult to help you.

Scissors

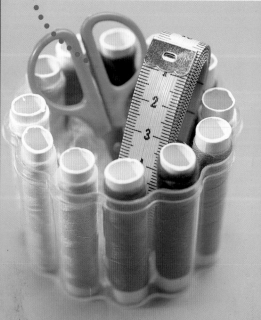

4

used to make the projects in this book.

Pins and needles

WOOL • For the knitting, woolly webs, and the cross-stitch, you will need yarn.

DARNING NEEDLE • If you are sewing with yarn, you will need a darning needle.

KNITTING NEEDLES • Knitting needles come in different sizes, so make sure you don't get ones that are too fat or thin.

SEWING NEEDLE • For sewing with thin thread, you will need a sewing needle with a small eye—not a darning needle. If you have trouble threading a needle, you can buy a cheap tool to make it easier.

PINS • Always pin material before you sew it.

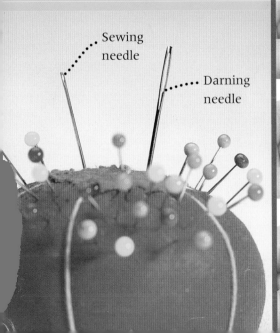

Sewing needle

Darning needle

Back stitch

This is a handy stitch to learn—it's quick yet strong and was used to stitch up Pirate Pete on page 16 to keep his filling from falling out. It's a bit like a doubled-up running stitch.

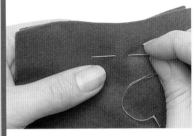

Knot the end of the thread. Push the needle down and up through the fabric.

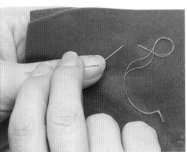

Pull the needle all the way through to the knot.

Place the needle between the knot and the dangling thread.

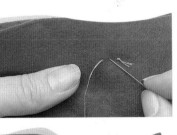

Bring the needle up ahead of the dangling thread.

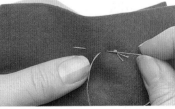

Repeat these steps and sew over a few stitches to finish off.

Fabrics

EMBROIDERY FABRIC • In order to make the cross-stitch patterns, you will have to buy special fabric called aida cloth. It has big holes that you can easily pull yarn through.

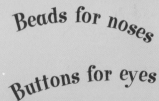

COTTON FABRIC • For Pirate Pete and friends, plain cotton, such as some old sheet material, is the best to use. Otherwise any old scraps of white cotton will do.

Beads for noses

Buttons for eyes

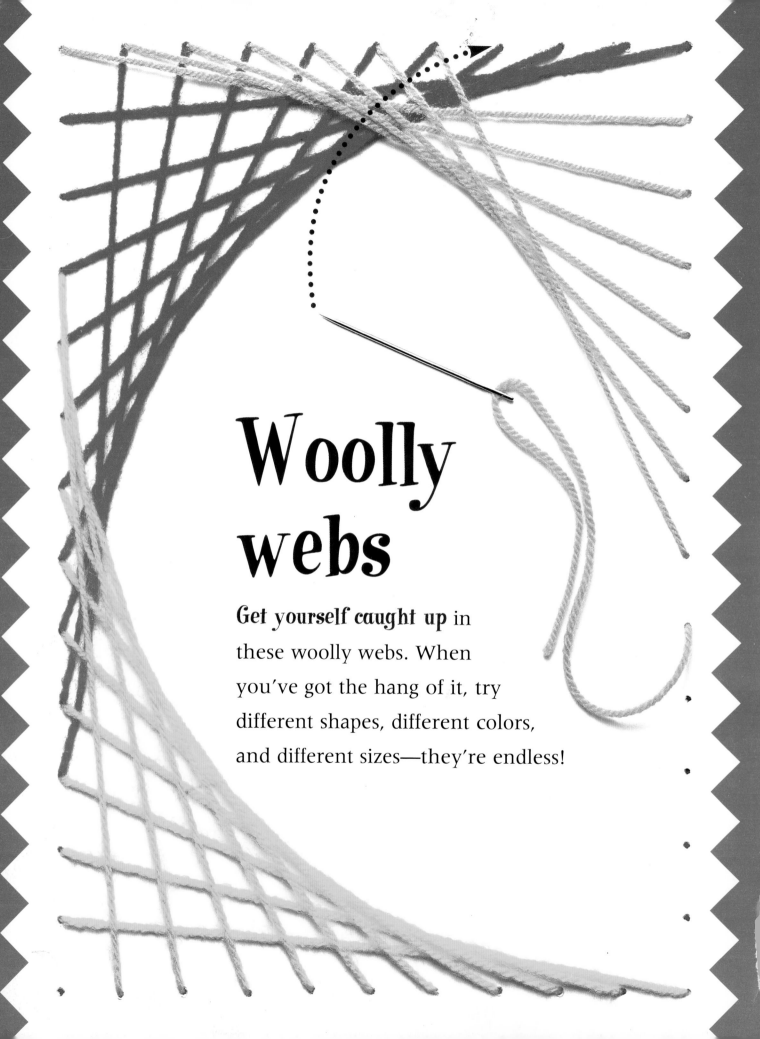

Woolly webs

Get yourself caught up in
these woolly webs. When
you've got the hang of it, try
different shapes, different colors,
and different sizes—they're endless!

Weaving kit

YARN

YARN AND DARNING NEEDLE

THICK PAPER OR POSTERBOARD

SCISSORS

PENCIL

RULER

SQUARE

Preparing the pattern

Draw a right angle on your paper of 5 in by 5 in (10 cm by 10 cm).

1. Draw a right angle

Weaving tips

• Use thick paper or posterboard. If the paper is too thin it will rip when you pull the thread through.

• For large patterns use yarn, but for smaller designs you could use lighter thread.

• When you get the hang of it, try using different-colored pieces of yarn. When you are really good, try different patterns.

• The most important thing is to EXPERIMENT and HAVE FUN.

Try the diamond design

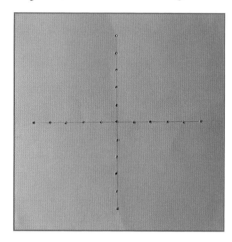

Start

The more holes you make, the bigger the pattern will be...

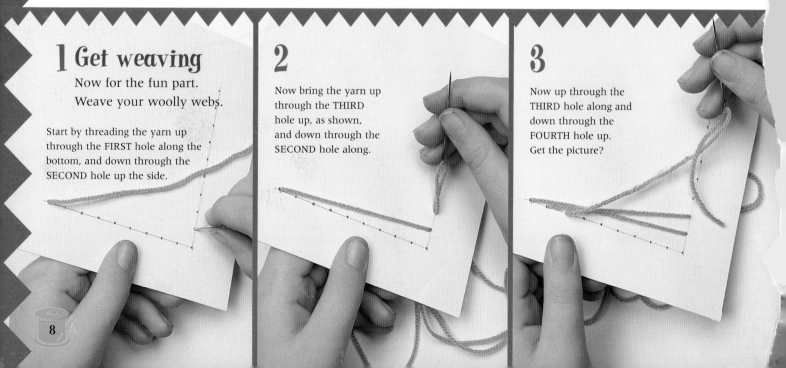

1 Get weaving

Now for the fun part. Weave your woolly webs.

Start by threading the yarn up through the FIRST hole along the bottom, and down through the SECOND hole up the side.

2

Now bring the yarn up through the THIRD hole up, as shown, and down through the SECOND hole along.

3

Now up through the THIRD hole along and down through the FOURTH hole up. Get the picture?

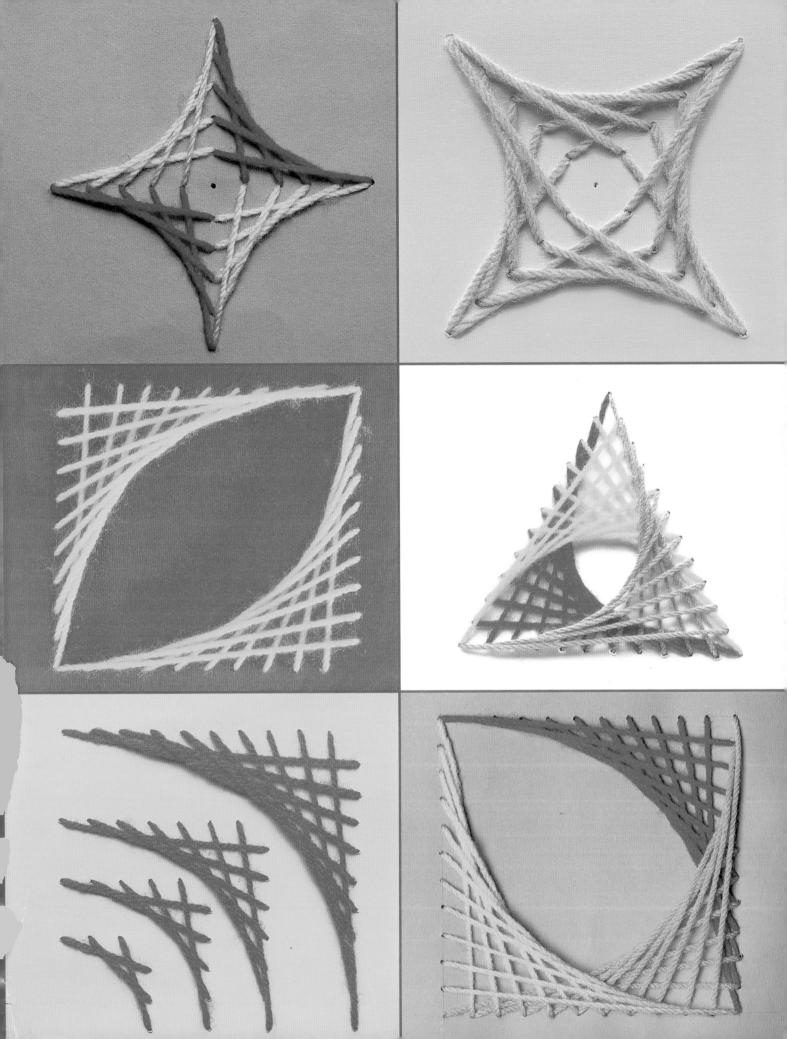

Mark dots along your lines, one every half inch (centimeter). You should end up with a row of 10 dots along and 10 dots up.

Take a darning needle and make a hole through each dot.

Place some cardboard underneath to protect the table.

Now thread some yarn onto the needle and knot the end.

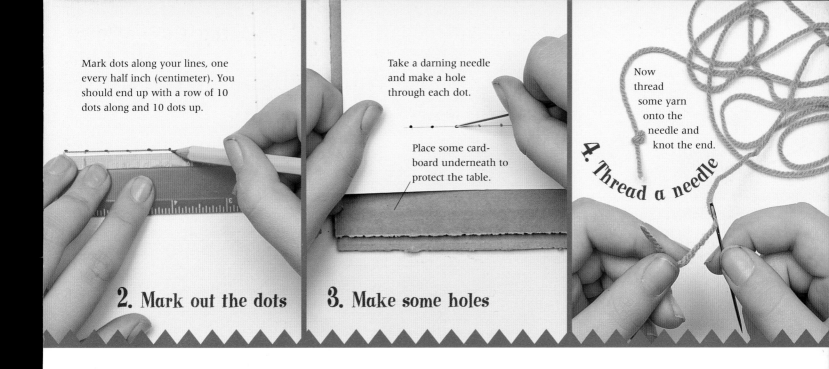

2. Mark out the dots

3. Make some holes

4. Thread a needle

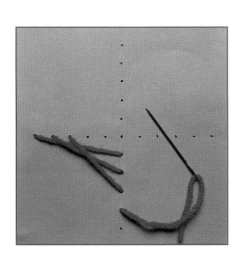

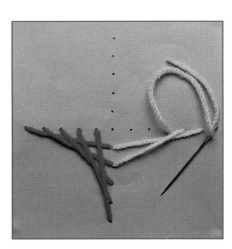

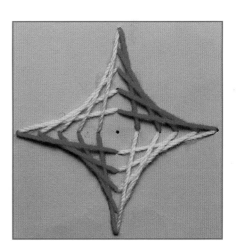

and remember, you can use each hole more than once—go on, weave a giant web!

4

Keep weaving in this pattern until you have no more holes to fill.

5

The last hole you use should be the top one, so thread down through it and stop.

6

Turn the paper over, tie a knot as close to the stitch as possible, and cut off the yarn end.

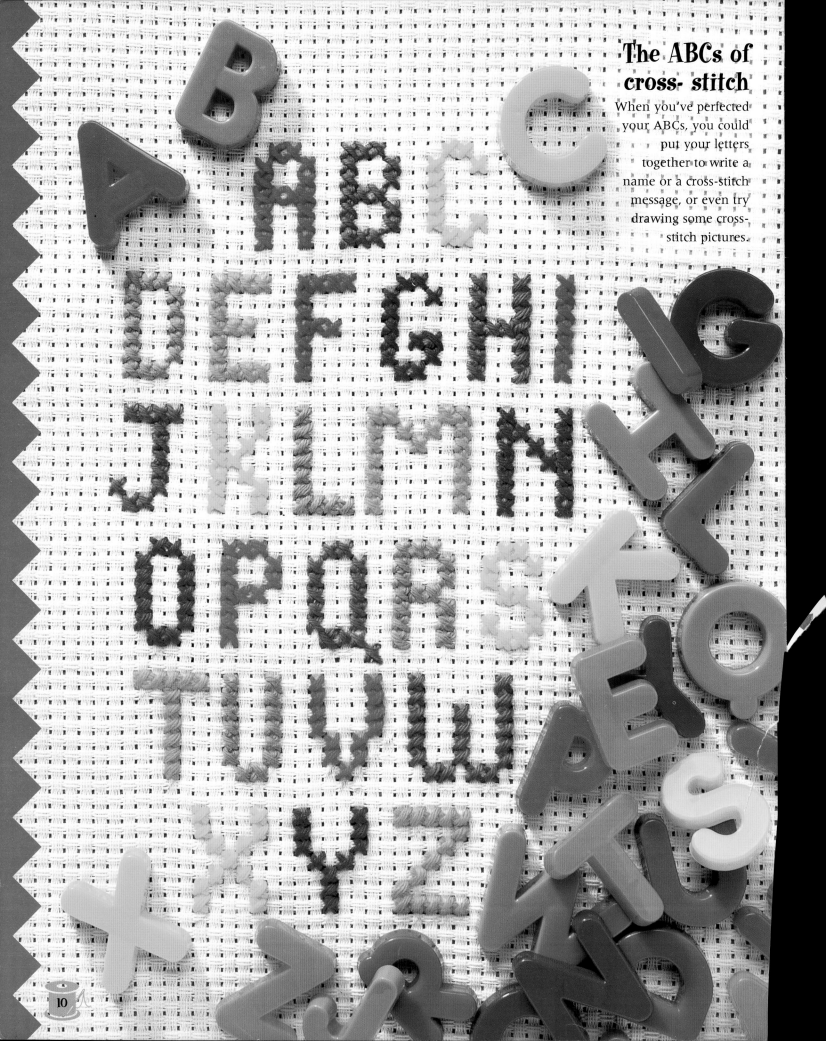

The ABCs of cross- stitch

When you've perfected your ABCs, you could put your letters together to write a name or a cross-stitch message, or even try drawing some cross-stitch pictures.

10

Cross-stitch

Simple samplers are as easy as A, B, C.
Crisscross, crisscross, and create pictures.

You will need

AIDA CLOTH • The large holes make it easy to see where to sew.

THREAD • Use anything from fine silk thread to wool yarn.

NEEDLE • A large-eyed darning needle is easy to thread and fits through the holes.

PENCIL • To mark out the squares.

Aida cloth *Darning needle*

Thread

Scissors

Following guide lines

• It helps to draw out the area you want to sew as small squares—each square is one cross-stitch.

• To keep your letters the same size, base them on the same number of squares across and up—for example, 7 squares down and 4 squares across.

• Remember, a curving part of a letter still has to be drawn using the squares.

Don't make the line too dark or it will show when sewn.

Pencil

Single stitch

For one stitch, use a short length of thread and don't forget to knot the end.

Stitches in a row

To sew a row, sew a few stitches one way, then go back the other way.

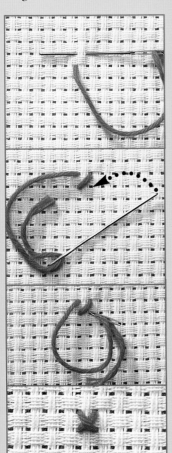

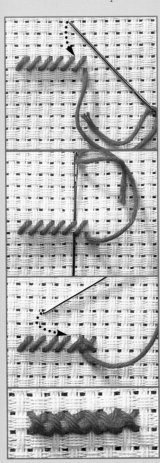

Back view and finishing off

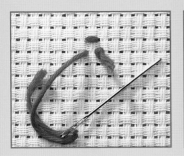

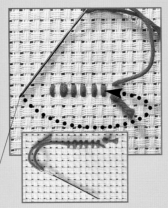

Finish a stitch on the back and thread it through some stitches to secure it.

A·B·C Cross-stitch letter squares

Once you have learned to cross-stitch, you can experiment with all sorts of different patterns and colors. Try these single letters. Cut a square of fabric about 18 holes by 18 holes. Draw on the areas in pencil, and stitch away.

Try fraying the edges of your work by pulling away the first few strands of the fabric.

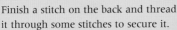

Pirate Pete

Yo, ho, ho, it's a pirate's life for me! How would you like to be drawn, sewn, and stuffed? That's how I'm made.

Land ho!

Shiver me beanbags

This jolly pirate is stuffed full of rice. You can use any dried food, such as lentils, popcorn, dried beans, or small pasta. Don't stuff it too full, however—it needs to be a bit floppy.

Follow the lines and dots

The hard line shows you where you cut the material, and the dotted line shows you where to sew.

Include these ears for cat shape.

Leave a space here to fill up your toy.

TRACING PAPER

PEN

SCISSORS

Pirate pattern

Sew along this line.

Cut out along this line.

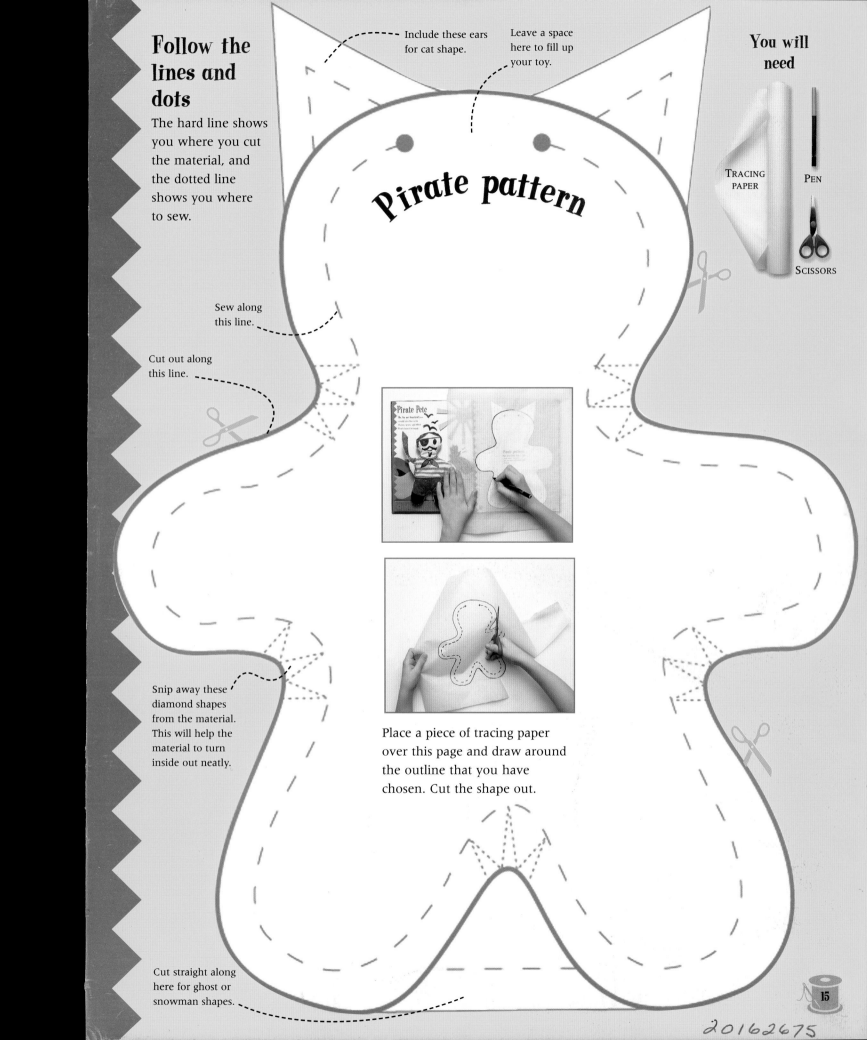

Snip away these diamond shapes from the material. This will help the material to turn inside out neatly.

Place a piece of tracing paper over this page and draw around the outline that you have chosen. Cut the shape out.

Cut straight along here for ghost or snowman shapes.

15

20162675

Meet the gang

"All aboard the Jolly Roger!"

shouts Pete to his crew. He couldn't sail his ship without his trusted beanbag friends. "Hoist the sails, raise the anchor, we're off to find the hidden treasure!"

Beanbag tips

Pete's pattern can be used to make the crew, too. Just add extra ears for the animals, yarn braids for the girls, and leave out the legs for the ghosts and snowman.

Whoo hoooo

Throw together Pete

Pirate Pete is ready to set sail

on the high seas. Use the template from page 15 to make Pirate Pete and go on to throw together his whole crew. "Ha, ha, me hearties!"

Your pirate kit

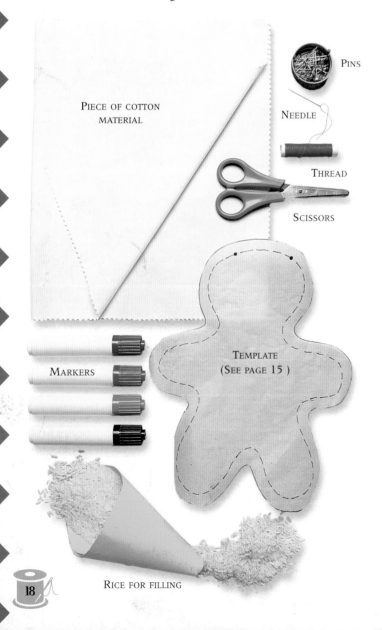

PINS

PIECE OF COTTON MATERIAL

NEEDLE

THREAD

SCISSORS

MARKERS

TEMPLATE (SEE PAGE 15)

RICE FOR FILLING

1

Cut out the shape

Lay the Pete template on a piece of material that is folded in half. Cut it out. You will now have two Pete shapes.

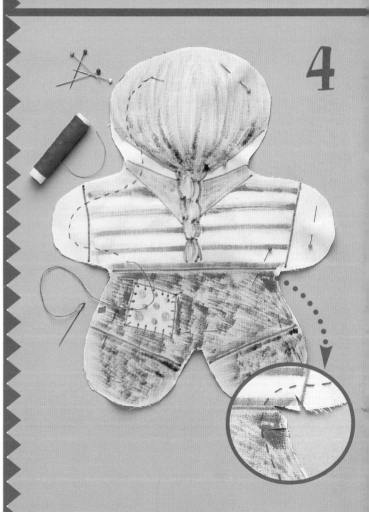

4

Sew all the way around

Use small stitches to sew around the pirate. Leave a small gap at the top.

2

Draw Pirate Pete

Color the front of Pete on one piece and draw the back of him on the other.

3

Pin the pieces together

Place the right sides of Pete together and pin them.

5

Turn him inside out

You should now see the right sides of Pete on the outside.

Curl a piece of paper into a tube funnel for easy filling.

When you have filled Pete, fold the open edges inward, pin them together, and sew the opening up.

6

Fill him up

Fill Pirate Pete up with a dried food, such as rice or beans, and sew him up!

Knitted pals

Ted sits and knits

a pal or two to play with,
complete with cozy hats.

Knitted hat

Hold on to your hats!

Easy knitting

Knitting is surprisingly simple, and once you get the hang of it, you can knit anything you want. All the knitted projects in this book are made only from knitted squares and rectangles—this makes them really easy! Start off with Ted, move on to his pals, then knit them all warm scarves and hats.

Off we go...

How to get started

You will need...

Casting on
This is how you get the stitches onto the needle. The pattern will tell you how many to cast on.

Tie the yarn to the needle, then pick up the yarn and twist it once.

Now twist the same piece again.

Slip the loop onto the needle.

Pull the yarn so that the stitch is quite tight.

Knitting stitches
Follow these instructions and just keep knitting and knitting and knitting!

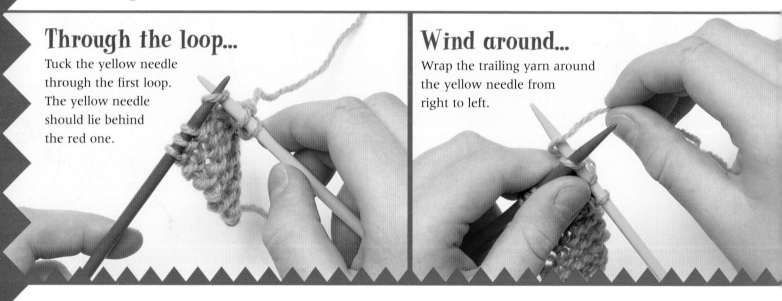

Through the loop...
Tuck the yellow needle through the first loop. The yellow needle should lie behind the red one.

Wind around...
Wrap the trailing yarn around the yellow needle from right to left.

Casting off
When you have have knitted enough rows, finish it by off by "casting off."

Knit two stitches as normal

On the yellow needle, take hold of the first stitch.

Pull the stitch right over the second and off the needle.

Knit another stitch and do the same again.

SCISSORS

BALL OF YARN

Row counter

This is a handy gadget that slides onto a needle. Each time you do a row, turn the the dial to show the number of rows you have done.

ROW COUNTER

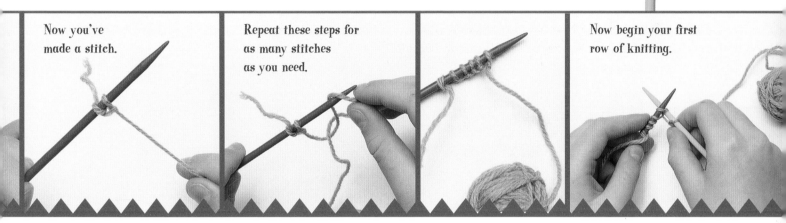

Now you've made a stitch.

Repeat these steps for as many stitches as you need.

Now begin your first row of knitting.

Under it goes...
Bring the yellow needle back up to the front with the loop still attached.

Off it comes
Release the stitch off the red needle, keeping it on the yellow one.

Keep going until you have one stitch left.

Snip the yarn.

Bring the end of the yarn through the loop and pull tight. This will secure it.

23

Watch me jump

Making Ted

Knit five pieces, sew them up, stuff them, and put them together. Hello, Ted!

1

Knit these five body pieces following the right number of rows and stitches.

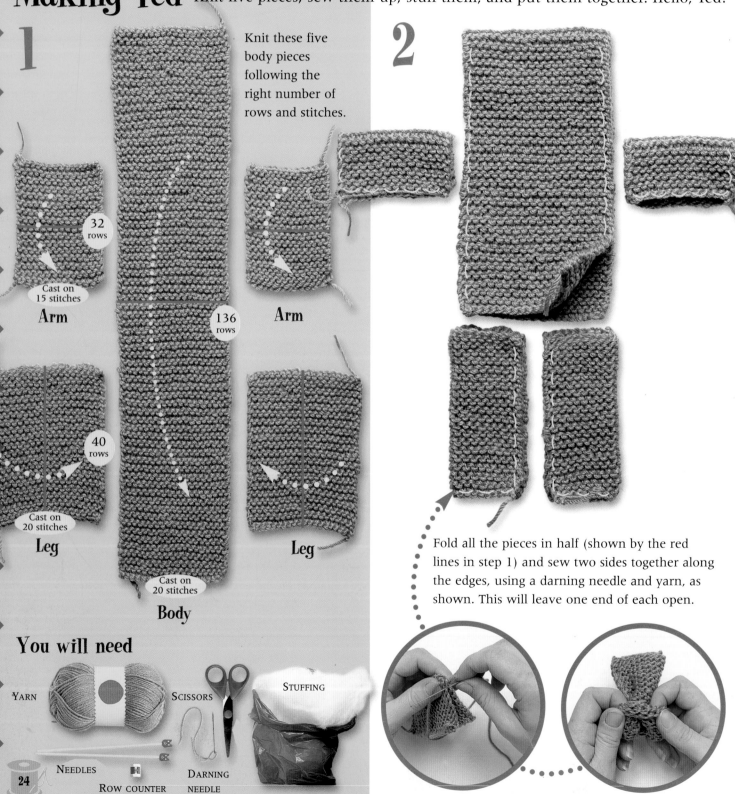

32 rows

Cast on 15 stitches

Arm

136 rows

Arm

40 rows

Cast on 20 stitches

Leg

Leg

Cast on 20 stitches

Body

You will need

YARN

SCISSORS

STUFFING

24

NEEDLES

ROW COUNTER

DARNING NEEDLE

2

Fold all the pieces in half (shown by the red lines in step 1) and sew two sides together along the edges, using a darning needle and yarn, as shown. This will leave one end of each open.

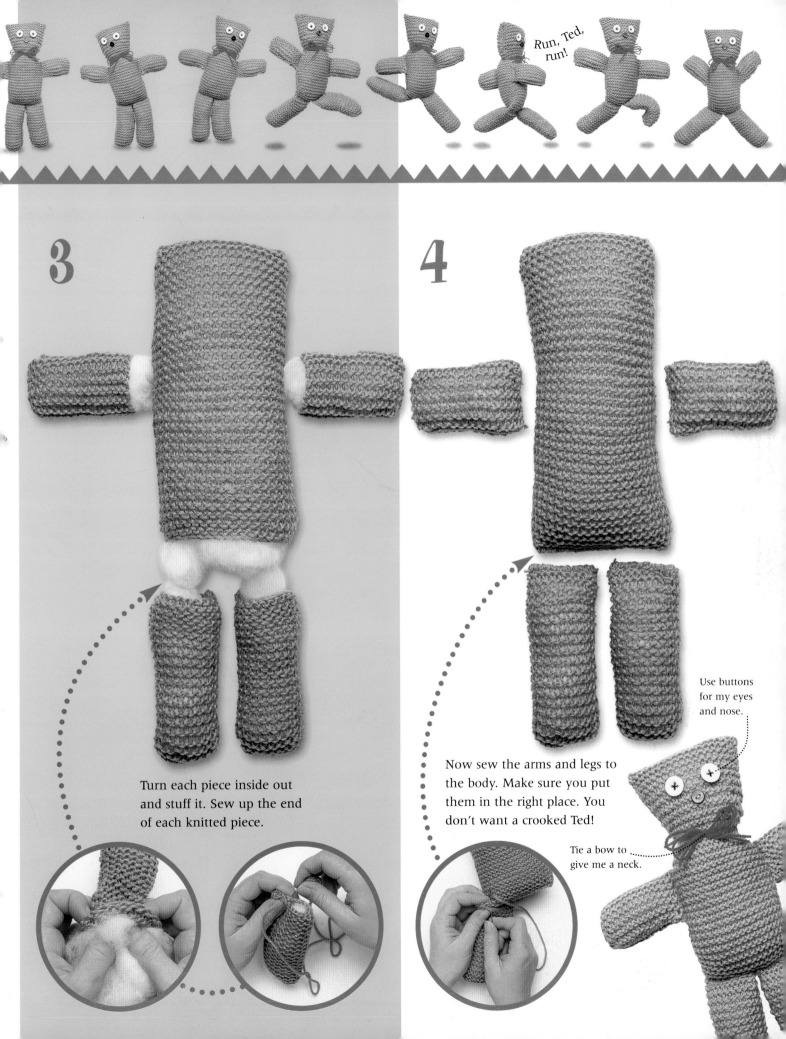

Run, Ted, run!

3

Turn each piece inside out and stuff it. Sew up the end of each knitted piece.

4

Now sew the arms and legs to the body. Make sure you put them in the right place. You don't want a crooked Ted!

Use buttons for my eyes and nose.

Tie a bow to give me a neck.

Ted's friends

You can't just make Ted, you need to make Ted's friends, too. And what happens if they get cold? Knit them scarves and hats, of course!

Make a friend for Ted

Ted's friend is very simple because he has wobbly legs.

26 rows

72 rows

Cast on 5 stitches

Arm

Body

Cast on 16 stitches

40 rows

Leg

Cast on 5 stitches

Making friends

Knit the five body pieces following the rows and stitches as shown. Fold the body in half, sew up two sides, turn it inside out, and stuff it—just like Ted on page 24. Then sew the body up and simply attach the arms and legs.

Beanie hats

Everyone needs a hat.

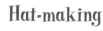

Hat-making

Ted's friend wants a hat. Cast on 54 stitches and knit 20 rows. Fold it in half, as above, and sew the top and side together. Put it on and turn up the bottom.

Sew on old buttons or beads for the eyes and nose.

A pom-pon for the hat

Cut out two discs from posterboard. Cut a hole in the middle of each.

2 in (5 cm) across

Put the discs together and tie a piece of yarn around them.

Use different colors.

Wind the yarn around and around through the middle and over the top. Stop when the discs are covered.

Put a pair of scissors between the discs and snip the yarn all around.

Tie a piece of yarn tightly around the pom-pon.

Take away the discs and fluff it up!

A fringe for the scarf

Knit Ted's long scarf as shown and finish if off nicely with a fringe.

Double up a piece of yarn and bring it up through the hole.

Stick a needle through the scarf above the first row.

Take the two ends, bring them up through the loop, and pull downward for the fringe. Repeat along the row.

140 rows

Cast on 12 stitches

Ted's hat

Ted's cozy hat is made by casting on 66 stitches and knitting 46 rows. Turn it up and finish it off with a bright pom-pon. Once you can make Ted's scarf and hat, why not try making full-size ones for friends? They make great gifts.

Marble paper

It's so good, the technique needs to be kept a secret!

Marble effects

Marble paper looks so
impressive that it will
astound your friends,
AND it's really easy to do.
Once you have made it,
you can wrap things in it,
cover things with it, use it
as a frame, write on it.
You'll impress everyone
you know with it!

The marble effect

Oil and water don't mix—that's how
the paint stays on the surface of the water—and
that's how it makes wiggly, marbly swirls on the
paper. If that doesn't make sense, don't worry;
just follow the instructions. You'll be amazed.

The paint mixture

Before you start, make the paint mixture.
Squeeze a blob of paint into a cup and add
four caps full of turpentine. Mix them
together. The paint will become very thin.

Ask an adult
to help mix the
paint with turpentine.

PAPER
TOWEL

WHITE PAPER

COCKTAIL
PICK

PAINT
CUPS

TURPENTINE

NEWSPAPER

BAKING TRAY
WITH WATER

OIL
PAINTS

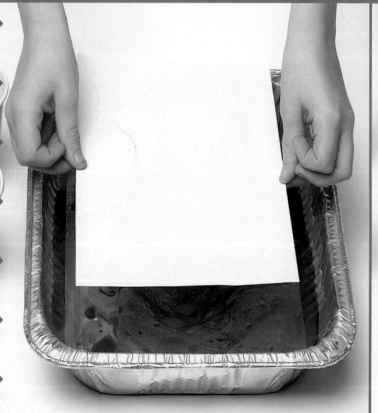

3 Lay the paper on it
Just let the paper float on the water.

4 Give it a push
Gently push the paper to help it make contact.

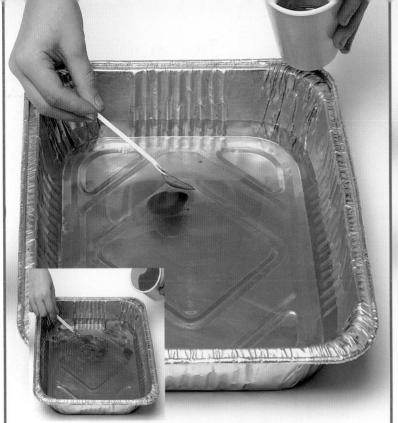

1 Add the paint to some water

Pour about 1 in (3 cm) of water into the tray. Add a small teaspoon of each color paint mixture.

2 Swirl the paint around

Dip a cocktail pick in and move it around in the mixture, but don't mix it!

5 Remove the paper

Pick up the corners and lift the paper out quickly.

6 Let it dry

Allow it to dry flat on newspaper.

Printing patterns

Take plain or colored paper and transform it into a frenzy of pattern. Go on, get printing!

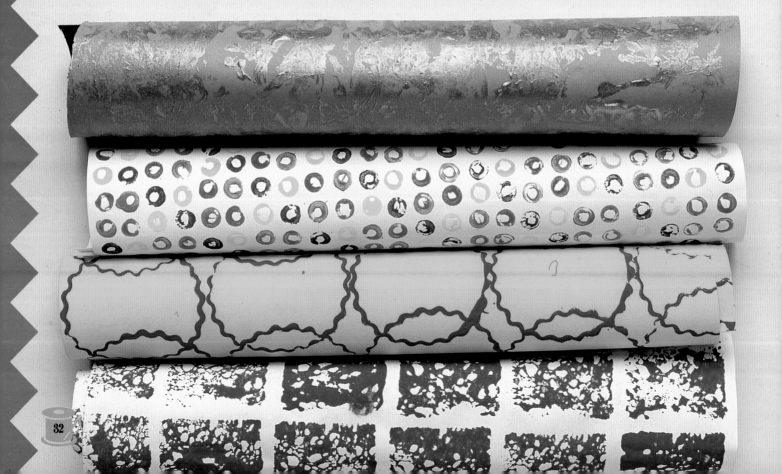

Making patterns

You will need to collect lots of paper to print on, such as brown packing paper, large sheets of plain white paper, or colored paper. The best paint to use is poster paint, but any paint you have will do. Try these babies' footprints using your hand—you could even use your own feet.

Babies' footprints

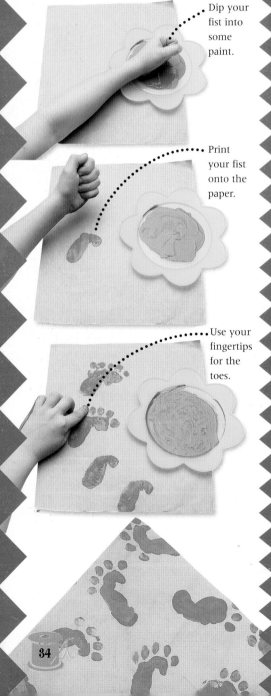

Dip your fist into some paint.

Print your fist onto the paper.

Use your fingertips for the toes.

Odds and ends

Search around the house for any items that you think would be good for printing. Remember to ask if you can cover these things in paint! Then dip them in the paint and press down on the paper.

Empty thread spools.

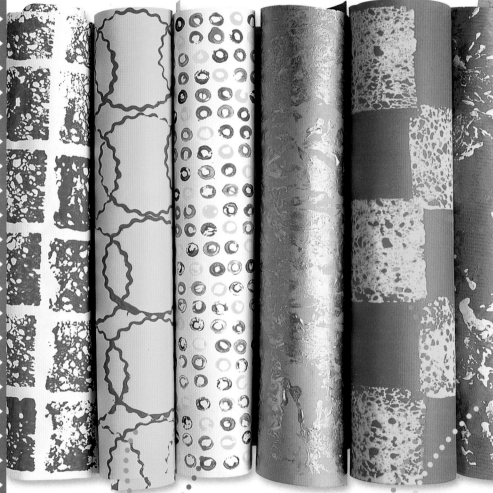

Pen end

Cookie cutter

Sponge

Scrunched-up plastic or paper bag.

Dip the spools into the paint.

Press down onto the paper.

Plastic letters

Carved-out carrot

Bubble wrap

Carved-out potato

Pen end

Brush

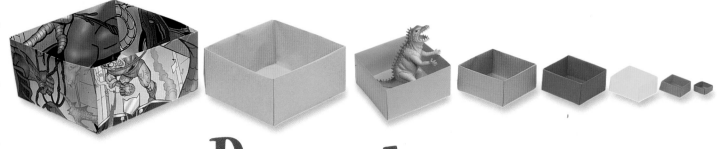

Paper boxes

What do you do if you need a box of a particular size? Simple: you make one yourself. And you can not only choose the size, you can choose the color, too. Try using wrapping paper or homemade printed paper.

Making a block box

As you make each fold, make sure you press the fold down firmly so that when you open it, you can see the crease.

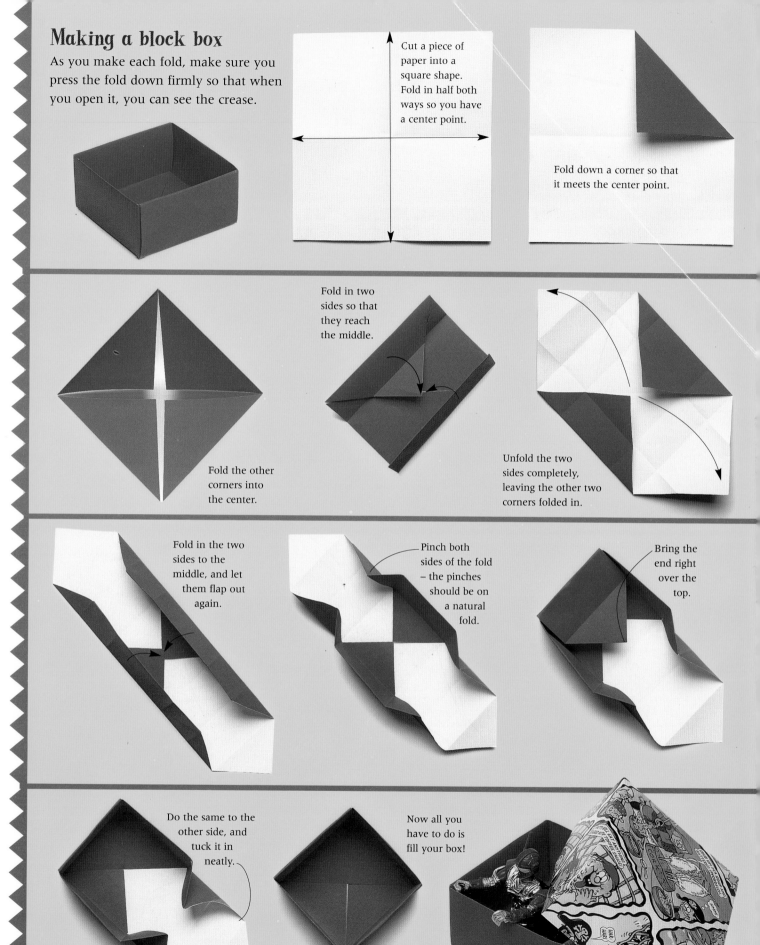

Cut a piece of paper into a square shape. Fold in half both ways so you have a center point.

Fold down a corner so that it meets the center point.

Fold in two sides so that they reach the middle.

Fold the other corners into the center.

Unfold the two sides completely, leaving the other two corners folded in.

Fold in the two sides to the middle, and let them flap out again.

Pinch both sides of the fold – the pinches should be on a natural fold.

Bring the end right over the top.

Do the same to the other side, and tuck it in neatly.

Now all you have to do is fill your box!

Use a slightly bigger piece of paper to make a lid.

A star box

Stuff your star full of candies and other delicious little fancies.

To start with... fold a square piece of paper... along these folds... then unfold them again.

Hold the top and bottom corners, and bring them together, making sure you tuck the two sides in.

The opening should be at the top.

It should be a diamond shape with two flaps in the middle.

Make sure the opening is at the top.

Fold one side along to the central fold.

Open up the small flap and press flat.

Make sure these two folds line up.

Tuck the left side of the small flap behind itself.

Now do the same to the other side.

Both sides should now look the same.

Turn it over so that the other side is showing.

Do the same with the flaps at the back.

The back should look exactly the same as the front.

Fold all four flaps down as far as they will go.

When you have folded two flaps down, pull the other two to the side and they will fold down, too.

Your box should start to open when you fold over the flaps.

With your hand underneath, push up the middle and it will miraculously turn into a box.

Neaten up the star flaps and FILL IT UP!

Try different sizes and colors. You could even try making them with your own printed paper.

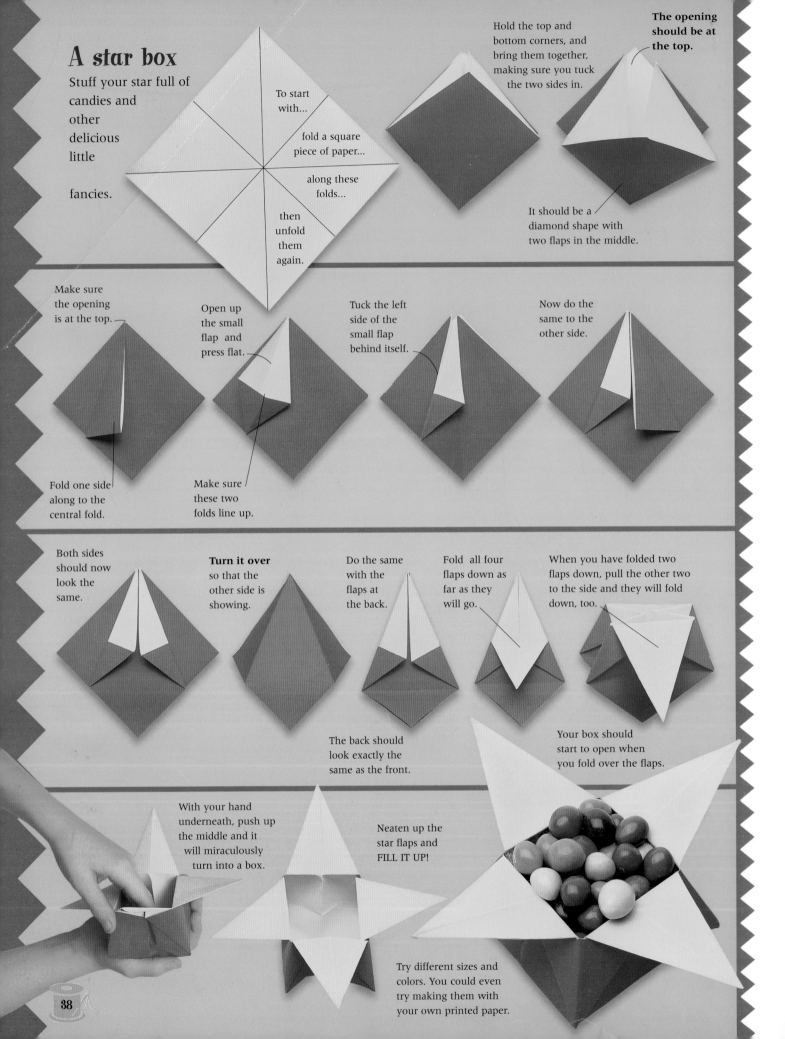

A galaxy of star boxes

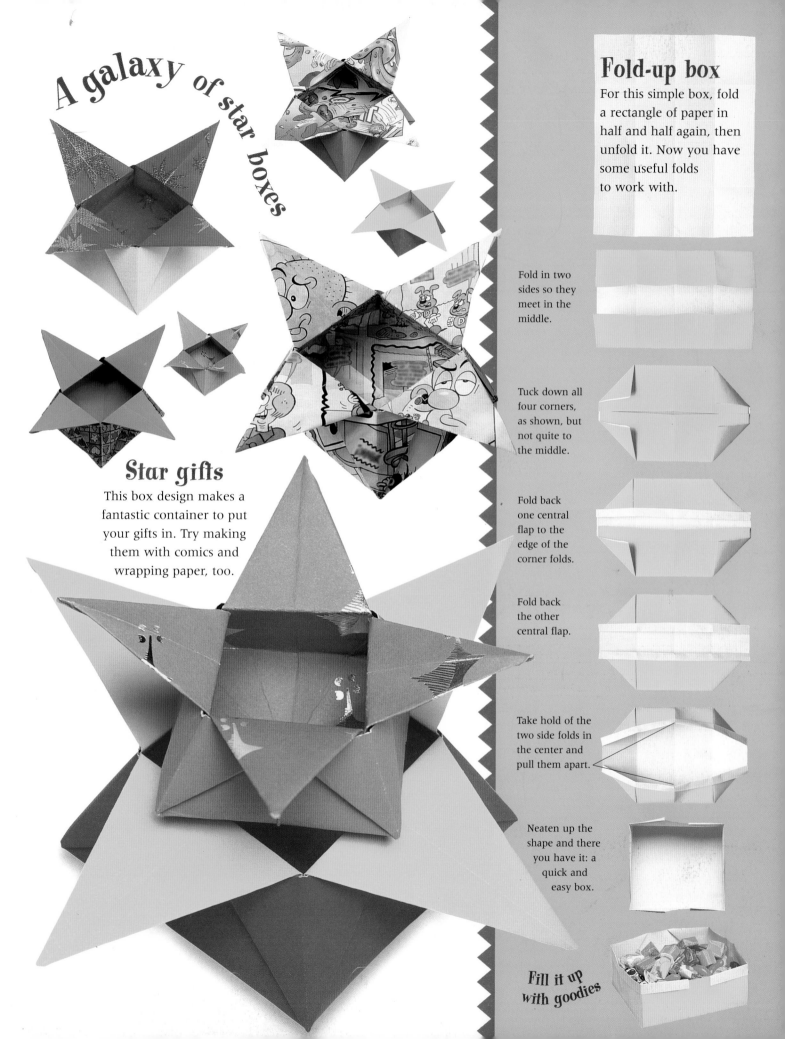

Star gifts

This box design makes a fantastic container to put your gifts in. Try making them with comics and wrapping paper, too.

Fold-up box

For this simple box, fold a rectangle of paper in half and half again, then unfold it. Now you have some useful folds to work with.

Fold in two sides so they meet in the middle.

Tuck down all four corners, as shown, but not quite to the middle.

Fold back one central flap to the edge of the corner folds.

Fold back the other central flap.

Take hold of the two side folds in the center and pull them apart.

Neaten up the shape and there you have it: a quick and easy box.

Fill it up with goodies

Paper roses

Fill a vase with home-grown tissue flowers and give a bunch to your mom.

Wild roses
Create a really wild, colorful bunch by mixing and matching the colors. If you want to make rose trees, see page 43 for instructions.

To make a rose

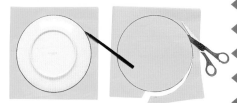

Take a piece of tissue paper and a plate about 6 in (15 cm) wide.

Draw around the plate and cut out six discs the same size.

Six tissue paper discs.

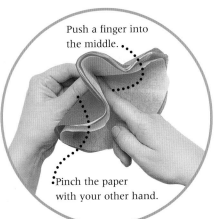

Push a finger into the middle.

Pinch the paper with your other hand.

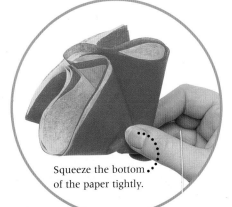

Squeeze the bottom of the paper tightly.

Tape the paper to a straw.

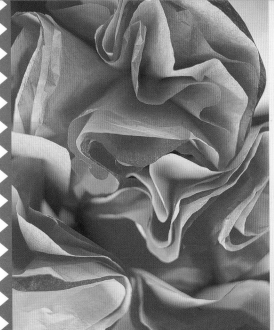

Rose trees

Rows of roses

SMALL PLATE

TISSUE PAPER

TAPE

PEN

SCISSORS

DRINKING STRAWS

Perfect petals

Finally, pull the layers apart carefully to fluff up the flower.

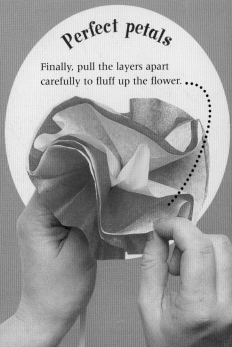

2 Now glue the other end of the zigzag.

1 Stick it down on one side.

3 Close the card.

4 Both sides should now be stuck on the inside so when you open it, the tutu will pop up.

Concertina ballerina
Fold a strip of poster-board into a zigzag as shown in step 1. Then glue one end.

5

Accordion cards

It's always great to get a card, especially if it's homemade. For someone really special, try making a 3-D card! Create the concertina ballerina.

Crafty cards
Using all the crafty ideas in this book.

Comic card

Fold up a comic page and snip a few holes out of it, open it up, and stick it on a card!

Woolly web card

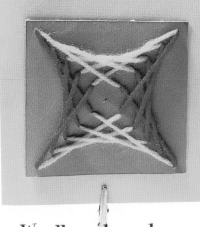

Your woolly webs are perfect patterns to stick onto cards.

Cross-stitch A B C

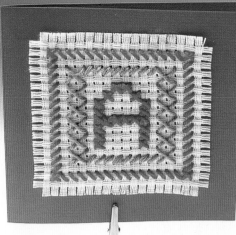

Use the initial of the person you are sending the card to and cross-stitch it.

Gift tags

Homemade tags finish off a present perfectly. Cut a tag out of posterboard, make a hole in the end, and tie a ribbon through it. Write on the tag or decorate it first.

Giving gifts

The tissue-paper roses on the previous page make lovely gifts. Pop one into a vase or turn several into a rose tree by putting them into a plastic cup. To do this, place a piece of sticky tack in the bottom of the cup and firmly push the straw stalk into it. Decorate the outside and give it as a present.

Three paper roses

Green tissue paper

Glue a piece of tissue paper around the cup and snip the edges.

Paper roses

The paper roses can also be stuck flat on a card or tag.

Special delivery

Cards and envelopes can be made from your own printed paper— or any paper you choose.

Aunt Daisy
4567 Garden Avenue
East Rosebud

Homemade envelopes

When you have made your cards, sometimes it's difficult to find the perfect-sized envelope to fit them. Your best bet is to make one yourself. You can even make it to match your card.

Measure your card to make sure it will fit in the envelope.

Take a square piece of paper and fold the left and right corners into the middle.

Fold the bottom corner up to the middle.

Fold the top flap down last, and when you have put a card inside, use a sticker to seal it.

To **Mom**

Dad

Grandma
123 Needle Street
Knittsville

Make envelopes out of
magazines, comics, wrapping
paper, or even brown paper.

For an even simpler
envelope, take a
rectangular piece of
paper and fold it into
three sections.

Unfold it and glue the
edges of the bottom
section.

Fold the top flap down.

Use a sticker to seal
the envelope down.

Write your
addresses on
sticky labels.

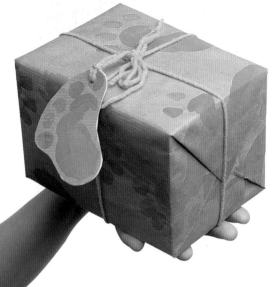

It's a wrap!

All wrapped up.
Give away your crafty projects as presents, wrapped in home-made paper with matching tags.

Tags

Cut out a shape and make a hole in the corner.

Wrap it up

Take a piece of your homemade paper, and put the present in the middle.

Fold one side over the top and hold it in place.

Fold the other side over and tape in place.

Tie a piece of ribbon or yarn through the hole.

Push the center of the paper down firmly.

Pull one side in and hold in place.

You could write a note on the tag...

To Mom

or print a pattern on it.

Fold the other side in.

Fold up the triangle shape and tape in place.

To match a tag to the footprint paper, cut around the print, make a hole, and tie some yarn through it.

Homemade paper
Now you have a gift all wrapped up in your homemade, personalized wrapping paper.

Thanks, Ted! Are these all from you?

Index

Acknowledgments

With thanks to...
Eleanor Bates, Charlotte Bull,
Billy Bull, and James Bull, for
craftily performing the arty
projects.

All images © Dorling Kindersley.
For further information, see
www.dkimages.com

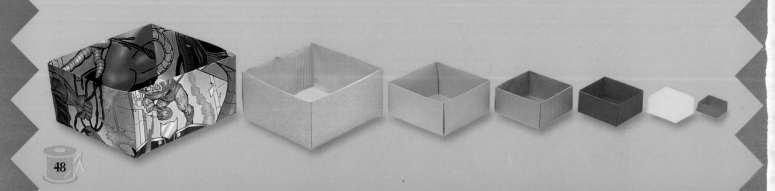